Poetry for Young People
Robert Louis Stevenson

Edited by Frances Schoonmaker
Illustrated by Lucy Corvino

Sterling Publishing Company, Inc.
New York

To Guy Haydon, Suwilanji Nakamba, Francis Mwita, and Matthews Chirwa
Nanjing, 1990

"The most beautiful adventures are not those we go to seek—"
—"An Inland Voyage," R.L.S.
— Frances Schoonmaker

To Dad, Mom, Kath, Chris, and Pru—
for many wonderful childhood memories
—Lucy Corvino

Library of Congress Cataloging-in-Publication Data
Stevenson, Robert Louis, 1850-1894.
[Poems. Selections]
Robert Louis Stevenson / edited by Frances Schoonmaker; illustrator, Lucy Corvino.
p.   cm. - (Poetry for young people)
Includes index.
Summary: An illustrated collection of thirty-two popular poems by Robert Louis Stevenson, mostly from "A Child's Garden of Verses." Includes an introduction about the poet's life and work.
ISBN 0-8069-4956-2
1. Children's poetry, Scottish. [1. Scottish poetry.] I. Schoonmaker, Frances.
II. Corvino, Lucy, ill. III. Title. IV. Series.
PR5489.A3   2000
821'.8-dc21   99-042991

5   7   9   10   8   6

Published by Sterling Publishing Co., Inc.
387 Park Avenue South, New York, N.Y. 10016
Text © 2000 by Frances Schoonmaker
Illustrations © 2000 by Lucy Corvino
The portrait on page 4: Courtesy of the Writers Museum, Edinburgh, Scotland
Distributed in Canada by Sterling Publishing
c/o Canadian Manda Group, One Atlantic Avenue, Suite 105
Toronto, Ontario, Canada M6K 3E7
Distributed in Great Britain and Europe by Chris Lloyd at Orca Book Services,
Stanley House, Fleets Lane, Poole BH15 3AJ England
Distributed in Australia by Capricorn Link (Australia) Pty Ltd.
P.O. Box 704, Windsor, NSW 2756 Australia
Printed in China
All rights reserved

Sterling ISBN 0-8069-4956-2

CONTENTS

INTRODUCTION

Robert Louis Stevenson always wanted to be a writer. He began "writing" letters when he was three years old. They were to his father, who was often away. His mother, Margaret, wrote them down for him. He never quit writing letters. Even when he was busy writing books, Louis—as his family called him—took time to write letters to family and friends. And no matter how far away he went, he found a way to mail them.

Thomas Stevenson, Louis's father, had his own ideas about young Stevenson's future. Thomas was a lighthouse engineer. His father before him had been one. In fact, Stevensons had set up the lighthouse system for all of Scotland. Everywhere boats went, they were guided by Stevenson lighthouses.

Grandfather Robert Stevenson became famous for building the Bell Rock lighthouse, off the coast of Scotland. Many ships had crashed there. People said it was impossible to put a lighthouse on Bell Rock, but Robert Stevenson figured out how to do it. Louis's father invented a special lens to make lighthouses shine even more brightly. Designing, improving, and inspecting lighthouses seemed to be in the Stevenson blood!

Louis wanted to please his parents. They were a very close and loving family, and he was their only child. So, when it was time to go to college, he went to the University of Edinburgh in Scotland, and studied engineering, but he paid little mind to his studies. Instead, he read books he wanted to read, and taught himself to write by studying how famous authors wrote.

After three and a half years of college, Louis knew that he just couldn't be an engineer. He finally had the courage to tell his father. Thomas was terribly disappointed, but he agreed that his son did not have to be an engineer. Instead, he said that young Louis could study law. Even though the study of law was not interesting to him, Louis finished law school. He even passed the bar examination to be a lawyer. But in his heart, he still wanted to write. By the time he was about twenty-five, he was spending all his time writing.

People must have thought Louis was a little odd. He was tall, thin, and often had a terrible cough. His eyes seemed to look right through people. He was a great talker and could tell a story like nobody else. Louis didn't mix with people who were friends of the Stevenson family. He liked to go his own way. He made friends with all kinds of people—rich and poor, educated and uneducated.

If he turned out to be an unusual young man, maybe it was because he had had an unusual childhood. Louis was born on November 13, 1850 in Edinburgh, Scotland. He was named Robert Lewis Balfour Stevenson for his grandfathers Robert Stevenson and Lewis Balfour. When he was about eighteen, he changed the spelling of Lewis to Louis. Later, he dropped Balfour because he hated having an extra initial in his name. He often signed his name R.L.S. in letters to family and friends.

As a child, Louis was often sick. In those days, many children died before they were five-years-old. People did not have the kind of medical care we have today. The Stevensons were very worried about Louis. As a baby, he was so sick that he needed a full-time nurse, or nanny, to help care for him. He often had to stay in bed. Being in bed all day was bad enough, but night-time was worse. When he wasn't awake from sickness, he had terrible nightmares. Many years later, he wrote to a friend about "the terrible long nights that I lay awake." He remembered the "hacking, exhausting cough." And he remembered "praying for sleep or morning from the bottom of my shaken little body."

It was his nurse, "Cummie," who rescued him. Alison Cunningham began working for the Stevensons when Louis was eighteen months old. "How well I remember her lifting me out of bed," he wrote, "carrying me to the window and showing me one or two lit windows up in Queen Street across the dark belt of gardens." Together they wondered if other nurses and sick little boys were also waiting for the morning. When he wrote a book of poems about his childhood, *A Child's Garden of Verses*, he dedicated it to her. Most of the poems here come from that book, which became one of his most famous. Louis wrote letters to Cummie for as long as she lived.

Not all of Louis's childhood memories were frightening. Both his father, Thomas Stevenson, and his mother, Margaret Isabella Balfour, came from large families. There were many children at family gatherings in Edinburgh and at holiday resorts in the summer. Louis's grandfather's home at Colington, just outside of Edinburgh, was often filled with grandchildren. The cousins all seemed to have great imaginations. They found many ways to play indoors and out. One of the things that made the Balfour home most exciting was Jane Whyte Balfour, Louis's aunt. She cared for the children when they were sick and taught them their school lessons. She never married. In Louis's opinion, she was the "Chief of our Aunts."

Louis was sick so often that he missed school for weeks and months at a time. When he couldn't be at school, he studied with a tutor. Hours and hours were spent in bed. There was no television or computer to entertain him. He had to find ways to amuse himself. Maybe that is why he had such a keen imagination. To him, the bed cover could be a magical land (see page 37). He could close his eyes and imagine himself to be in "The Little Land" full of little people in a flower forest (see page 34). And he knew how the garden changed from night to day (see page 26). His world of adventures found its way into his poems for children and into the wonderful adventure stories that he wrote.

In spite of his poor health, Stevenson was an adventurer. As a young man, he went with his father on trips to inspect lighthouses. Once when he and his father were on the shore, they waved a handkerchief at a boat to come ashore and pick them up. He wrote to his mother that it "made me remember many old daydreams when it was my only wish to be a pirate or a smuggler." This daydream found its way into a story about pirates. The story, which first appeared one chapter at a time in a paper called *Young Folks*, was *Treasure Island*. It became one of his most popular books. He had fun writing it, too. While he was working on it, Louis wrote a friend, "No writing, just drive along as the words come and the pen will scratch!"

Stevenson went on canoe trips and camped out when he could. He was returning from a canoe trip when he met the woman he was to marry. One evening, some friends were sitting around the table of an old inn in the lamplight. Stevenson saw them through the window. Frances Matilda Vandegrift Osbourne was there, too. The minute he saw her, Louis was in love. One story has it that when he saw his friends and Fanny, he jumped through the open window. In any case, everyone was surprised and happy to see him. Soon he and Fanny became friends.

Fanny was married. She was an American, eleven years older than Louis. She had a son and a daughter. Fanny was no stranger to adventure. She had travelled west with her restless husband. She made a home in silver mining camps. She had learned how to ride a horse, shoot a revolver, and fire a rifle. She also loved art and gardening. Before meeting Louis, she had decided to leave her husband. She and the children were living in Paris, where she and her daughter studied art.

Four years later Fanny was back in California. Louis took a steamship to the United States; he wanted to gather information for his writing, and he wanted to see Fanny. Instead of taking a comfortable cabin on the ship, he went as an emigrant. That way he could save money and collect material to write about. After the long trip across the Atlantic Ocean, he took a train from New York to California. He had to change trains many times. Sometimes he rode on top of a railroad car along with other emigrants. Even then, he wrote letters. He told one friend, "my present station on the waggon* roof, though airy compared to the cars, is both dirty and insecure." He could see the train tracks stretching out before and behind. He washed from a tin bowl he shared with four other people, and he ate very little.

Stevenson's spelling.

When the trip came to an end, Louis camped out. He was in the mountains along the California coast, and again he became sick. Some ranchers found him at his camp. They took him to an angora goat ranch. There they took care of him. He stayed on the ranch until he was strong enough to travel to San Francisco, where Fanny lived. Even while he was in bed, Louis wrote letters to friends and worked on notes for his stories.

When he was well enough, Louis and Fanny were married. But his health became worse. At some point in his life, his weak lungs had developed tuberculosis. The Stevensons spent much of their time looking for the best location for him to live and work. For several years, the family, including Fanny's two children, lived in England. That was when three of his most famous works were published. One was another pirate story, *Kidnapped*. Another was *A Child's Garden of Verses*. The third was a nightmare! That is, it began as a nightmare.

One night Louis was so restless that Fanny woke him. Instead of being happy to be out of the nightmare, he was cross. "Why did you wake me?" he asked. "I was dreaming a fine bogey tale." Three days later he had written *The Strange Case of Dr. Jekyll and Mr. Hyde*. He tore up the first version and worked for three more days, until the second draft was done. Within a few weeks the book was ready to be published.

The rainy English climate was not good for Louis, so they went to the South Seas where it was warmer. One of the places they visited was Hawaii. There, Louis became friends with David Kalakaua, the last King of Hawaii. King Kalakaua wanted the Stevensons to stay in Hawaii, but they kept travelling until they found the ideal spot. It was on the Samoan island of Upolu. The native Samoans loved Louis. They called him "Tusitala," or the teller of tales.

The Stevensons lived in Samoa for the last four years of Louis's life. When he died, at age 44, he was buried at the top of a nearby mountain. Many years before, he had written to a friend, "When I die of consumption (tuberculosis), you can put that upon my tomb." He had a sketch of what he wanted, including two lines of a poem, "Home is the sailor, home from the sea, And the hunter home from the hill." Then he teased, "The verses are from a beayootiful poem by me." The whole poem, "Requiem," was put on his tomb (it's on page 47).

Louis was near death so many times, it was natural for him to think about his grave. In writing to his friend, he explained that he wanted people who paused and read his grave marker to ask themselves, "Can I make someone happier this day before I lie down to sleep?" Few people will ever stop by his grave because it is so far away. But Robert Louis Stevenson's poems and adventure stories have made people happy for many years.

Quotations from letters are from Ernest Mehew, Selected Letters of Robert Louis Stevenson. *New Haven, London: Yale University Press, 1997.*

TIME TO RISE

A birdie with a yellow bill
Hopped upon the window sill,
Cocked his shining eye and said:
"Ain't you 'shamed, you sleepy-head?"

BED IN SUMMER

In winter I get up at night
And dress by yellow candle-light.
In summer, quite the other way,
I have to go to bed by day.

I have to go to bed and see
The birds still hopping on the tree,
Or hear the grown-up people's feet
Still going past me in the street.

And does it not seem hard to you,
When all the sky is clear and blue,
And I should like so much to play,
To have to go to bed by day?

HAPPY THOUGHT

The world is so full of a number of things,
I'm sure we should all be as happy as kings.

WHOLE DUTY OF CHILDREN

A child should always say what's true
And speak when he is spoken to,
And behave mannerly at table;
At least as far as he is able.

SINGING

Of speckled eggs the birdie sings
    And nests among the trees;
The sailor sings of ropes and things
    In ships upon the seas.

The children sing in far Japan,
    The children sing in Spain;
The organ with the organ man
    Is singing in the rain.

RAIN

The rain is raining all around,
    It falls on field and tree,
It rains on the umbrellas here,
    And on the ships at sea.

SUMMER SUN

Great is the sun, and wide he goes
Through empty heaven without repose;
And in the blue and glowing days
More thick than rain he showers his rays.

Though closer still the blinds we pull
To keep the shady parlour cool,
Yet he will find a chink or two
To slip his golden fingers through.

The dusty attic spider-clad
He, through the keyhole, maketh glad;
And through the broken edge of tiles,
Into the laddered hay-loft smiles.

Meantime his golden face around
He bares to all the garden ground,
And sheds a warm and glittering look
Among the ivy's inmost nook.

Above the hills, along the blue,
Round the bright air with footing true,
To please the child, to paint the rose,
The gardener of the World, he goes.

repose—*rest*

THE SWING

How do you like to go up in a swing,
  Up in the air so blue?
Oh, I do think it the pleasantest thing
  Ever a child can do!

Up in the air and over the wall,
  Till I can see so wide,
Rivers and trees and cattle and all
  Over the countryside—

Till I look down on the garden green,
  Down on the roof so brown—
Up in the air I go flying again,
  Up in the air and down!

AT THE SEA-SIDE

When I was down beside the sea
A wooden spade they gave to me
   To dig the sandy shore.
My holes were empty like a cup,
In every hole the sea came up,
   Till it could come no more.

A VISIT FROM THE SEA

Far from the loud sea beaches
    Where he goes fishing and crying,
Here in the inland garden
    Why is the sea-gull flying?

Here are no fish to dive for;
    Here is the corn and lea;
Here are the green trees rustling.
    Hie away home to sea!

Fresh is the river water
    And quiet among the rushes;
This is no home for the sea-gull
    But for the rooks and thrushes.

Pity the bird that has wandered!
    Pity the sailor ashore!
Hurry him home to the ocean,
    Let him come here no more!

High on the sea-cliff ledges
    The white gulls are trooping and crying,
Here among rooks and roses,
    Why is the sea-gull flying?

lea—*grassy land or pasture*
hie—*to go quickly*
rook—*a bird, like a crow*
thrush—*a bird*

WHERE GO THE BOATS?

Dark brown is the river,
   Golden is the sand.
It flows along for ever,
   With trees on either hand.

Green leaves a-floating,
   Castles of the foam,
Boats of mine a-boating—
   Where will all come home?

On goes the river
   And out past the mill,
Away down the valley,
   Away down the hill.

Away down the river,
   A hundred miles or more,
Other little children
   Shall bring my boats ashore.

KEEPSAKE MILL

Over the borders, a sin without pardon,
　　Breaking the branches and crawling below,
Out through the breach in the wall of the garden,
　　Down by the banks of the river we go.

Here is the mill with the humming of thunder,
　　Here is the weir with the wonder of foam,
Here is the sluice with the race running under—
　　Marvellous places, though handy to home!

Sounds of the village grow stiller and stiller,
　　Stiller the note of the birds on the hill;
Dusty and dim are the eyes of the miller,
　　Deaf are his ears with the moil of the mill.

Years may go by, and the wheel in the river
　　Wheel as it wheels for us children, today,
Wheel and keep roaring and foaming for ever
　　Long after all of the boys are away.

Home from the Indies and home from the ocean,
　　Heroes and soldiers we all shall come home;
Still we shall find the old mill wheel in motion,
　　Turning and churning that river to foam.

You with the bean that I gave when we quarrelled,
　　I with your marble of Saturday last,
Honoured and old and all gaily apparelled,
　　Here we shall meet and remember the past.

breach—*a break*

weir—*a dam in a stream, made to raise the water level or send the*
　　　water in another direction

sluice—*a place made for water from a stream can pass through or be*
　　　stopped from flowing

moil—*confusion, turmoil*

apparelled—*clothed*

17

TRAVEL

I should like to rise and go
Where the golden apples grow;—
Where below another sky
Parrot islands anchored lie,
And, watched by cockatoos and goats,
Lonely Crusoes building boats;—
Where in sunshine reaching out
Eastern cities, miles about,
Are with mosque and minaret
Among sandy gardens set,
And the rich goods from near and far
hang for sale in the bazaar;—
Where the Great Wall round China goes,
And on one side the desert blows,
And with bell and voice and drum,
Cities on the other hum;—
Where are forests, hot as fire,
Wide as England, tall as a spire,
Full of apes and cocoa-nuts
And the negro hunters' huts;—
Where the knotty crocodile
Lies and blinks in the Nile,
And the red flamingo flies
Hunting fish before his eyes;—
Where in jungles, near and far,
Man-devouring tigers are,
Lying close and giving ear
Lest the hunt be drawing near,

Or a comer-by be seen
Swinging in a palanquin;—
Where among the desert sands
Some deserted city stands,
All its children, sweep and prince,
Grown to manhood ages since,
Not a foot in street or house,
Not a stir of child or mouse,
And when kindly falls the night,
In all the town no spark of light.
There I'll come when I'm a man
With a camel caravan;
Light a fire in the gloom
Of some dusty dining-room;
See the pictures on the walls,
Heroes, fights and festivals;
And in a corner find the toys
Of the old Egyptian boys.

Crusoes—*Robinson Crusoe is a character in a book who was
stranded all alone on an island.*

mosque—*a temple or building used for worship by Muslims*

minaret—*a tower of a mosque; used for calling Muslims to prayer*

bazaar—*a place where things are sold from rows of little shops or
stalls*

palanquin—*a form of transportation, usually for one person; it
looks like a little enclosed box on long poles that rest
on the shoulders of those who carry it.*

caravan—*a group travelling in line*

THE SUN'S TRAVELS

The sun is not a-bed, when I
At night upon my pillow lie;
Still round the earth his way he takes,
And morning after morning makes.

While here at home, in shining day,
We round the sunny garden play,
Each little Indian sleepy-head
Is being kissed and put to bed.

And when at eve I rise from tea,
Day dawns beyond the Atlantic Sea;
And all the children in the West
Are getting up and being dressed.

THE LAND OF NOD

From breakfast on through all the day
At home among my friends I stay,
But every night I go abroad
Afar into the land of Nod.

All by myself I have to go,
With none to tell me what to do—
All alone beside the streams
And up the mountain-sides of dreams.

The strangest things are there for me,
Both things to eat and things to see,
And many frightening sights abroad
Till morning in the land of Nod.

Try as I like to find the way,
I never can get back by day,
Nor can remember plain and clear
The curious music that I hear.

ESCAPE AT BEDTIME

The lights from the parlour and kitchen shone out
    Through the blinds and the windows and bars;
And high overhead and all moving about,
    There were thousands of millions of stars.
There ne'er were such thousands of leaves on a tree,
    Nor of people in church or the Park,
As the crowds of the stars that looked down upon me,
    And that glittered and winked in the dark.

The Dog, and the Plough, and the Hunter, and all
    And the star of the sailor, and Mars,
These shone in the sky, and the pail by the wall
    Would be half full of water and stars.
They saw me at last, and they chased me with cries,
    And they soon had me packed into bed;
But the glory kept shining and bright in my eyes,
    And the stars going round in my head.

The Dog, the Plough, and the Hunter—*groups of stars
called constellations.*

22

YOUNG NIGHT-THOUGHT

All night long and every night,
When my mamma puts out the light,
I see the people marching by,
And plain as day, before my eye.

Armies and emperors and kings,
All carrying different kinds of things,
And marching in so grand a way,
You never saw the like by day.

So fine a show was never seen
At the great circus on the green;
For every kind of beast and man
Is marching in that caravan.

At first they move a little slow,
But still the faster on they go,
And still beside them close I keep
Until we reach the town of Sleep.

caravan—*a group travelling in line*

NIGHT AND DAY

When the golden day is done,
   Through the closing portal,
Child and garden, flower and sun,
   Vanish all things mortal.

As the blinding shadows fall,
   As the rays diminish,
Under evening's cloak they all
   Roll away and vanish.

Garden darkened, daisy shut,
   Child in bed, they slumber—
Glow-worm in the highway rut,
   Mice among the lumber.

In the darkness houses shine,
   Parents move with candles;
Till on all the night divine
   Turns the bedroom handles.

Till at last the day begins
   In the east a-breaking,
In the hedges and the whins
   Sleeping birds a-waking.

In the darkness shapes of things,
   Houses, trees, and hedges,
Clearer grow; and sparrow's wings
   Beat on window ledges.

These shall wake the yawning maid;
    She the door shall open—
Finding dew on garden glade
    And the morning broken.

There my garden grows again
    Green and rosy painted,
As at eve behind the pane
    From my eyes it fainted.

Just as it was shut away,
    Toy-like, in the even,
Here I see it glow with day
    Under glowing heaven.

Every path and every plot,
    Every bush of roses,
Every blue forget-me-not
    Where the dew reposes,

"Up!" they cry, "the day is come
    On the smiling valleys:
We have beat the morning drum;
    Playmate, join your allies!"

portal—*a door or entrance*
diminish—*to make less, or smaller, little by little*
glowworm—*another word for fire-fly*
highway rut—*the marks made on a road by*
                many wheels over time
whins—*bent grasses*
even—*evening*
reposes—*rests*

FOREIGN LANDS

Up into the cherry tree
Who should climb but little me?
I held the trunk with both my hands
And looked abroad on foreign lands.

I saw the next door garden lie,
Adorned with flowers, before my eye,
And many pleasant places more
That I had never seen before.

I saw the dimpling river pass
And be the sky's blue looking-glass;
The dusty roads go up and down
With people tramping in to town.

If I could find a higher tree,
Farther and farther I should see,
To where the grown-up river slips
Into the sea among the ships,

To where the roads on either hand
Lead onward into fairy land,
Where all the children dine at five,
And all the playthings come alive.

adorned—*decorated*

MY SHADOW

I have a little shadow that goes in and out with me,
And what can be the use of him is more than I can see.
He is very, very like me from the heels up to the head;
And I see him jump before me, when I jump into my bed.

The funniest thing about him is the way he likes to grow—
Not at all like proper children, which is always very slow;
For he sometimes shoots up taller like an india-rubber ball,
And he sometimes gets so little that there's none of him at all.

He hasn't got a notion of how children ought to play,
And can only make a fool of me in every sort of way.
He stays so close behind me, he's a coward you can see;
I'd think shame to stick to nursie as that shadow sticks to me!

One morning, very early, before the sun was up,
I rose and found the shining dew on every buttercup;
But my lazy little shadow, like an arrant sleepy-head,
Had stayed at home behind me and was fast asleep in bed.

arrant—*extreme*

AUTUMN FIRES

In the other gardens
   And all up the vale,
From the autumn bonfires
   See the smoke trail!

Pleasant summer over
   And all the summer flowers,
The red fire blazes,
   The gray smoke towers.

Sing a song of seasons!
   Something bright in all!
Flowers in the summer,
   Fires in the fall!

vale—*a valley or dale*

31

PIRATE STORY

Three of us afloat in the meadow by the swing,
    Three of us aboard in the basket on the lea.
Winds are in the air, they are blowing in the spring,
    And waves are on the meadow like the waves there are at sea.

Where shall we adventure, today that we're afloat,
    Wary of the weather and steering by a star?
Shall it be to Africa, a-steering of the boat,
    To Providence, or Babylon, or off to Malabar?

Hi! but here's a squadron a-rowing on the sea—
    Cattle on the meadow a-charging with a roar!
Quick, and we'll escape them, they're as mad as they can be,
    The wicket is the harbour and the garden is the shore.

lea—*grassy land or pasture*
wary—*careful to avoid danger*
squadron—*two or more groups of boats or vessels in a navy*
wicket—*a small gate or door*

THE LITTLE LAND

When at home at last I sit
And am very tired of it,
I have just to shut my eyes
To go sailing through the skies—
To go sailing far away
To the pleasant Land of Play;
To the fairy land afar
Where the Little People are;
Where the clover-tops are trees,
And the rain-pools are the seas,
And the leaves like little ships,
Sail about on tiny trips;
And above the daisy tree
     Through the grasses,
High o'erhead the Bumble Bee
     Hums and passes.

In that forest to and fro
I can wander, I can go;
See the spider and the fly,
And the ants go marching by
Carrying parcels with their feet
Down the green and grassy street.
I can in the sorrel sit
Where the ladybird alit.
I can climb the jointed grass
     And on high
See the greater swallows pass
     In the sky,
And the round sun rolling by
Heeding no such things as I.

Through that forest I can pass
Till, as in a looking glass,
Humming fly and daisy tree
And my tiny self I see,
Painted very clear and neat

On the rain-pool at my feet.
Should a leaflet come to land
Drifting near to where I stand,
Straight I'll board that tiny boat
Round the rain-pool sea to float.

Little thoughtful creatures sit
On the grassy coasts of it;
Little things with lovely eyes
See me sailing with surprise.
Some are clad in armour green—
(These have sure to battle been!)—
Some are pied with ev'ry hue,
Black and crimson, gold and blue;
Some have wings and swift are gone;—
But they all look kindly on.

When my eyes I once again
Open, and see all things plain:
High bare walls, great bare floor;
Great big knobs on drawer and door;
Great big people perched on chairs,
Stitching tucks and mending tears,
Each a hill that I could climb,
And talking nonsense all the time—
　　O dear me,
　　That I could be
A sailor on the rain-pool sea,
A climber in the clover tree,
And just come back a sleepy-head,
Late at night to go to bed.

sorrel—*a leafy plant with sour juice*
alit—*landed*
ladybird—*another name for lady bug*
pied—*two or more colors in blotches or uneven*
　　　speckles
hue—*color or shade of a color*

THE LAND OF COUNTERPANE

When I was sick and lay a-bed,
I had two pillows at my head,
And all my toys beside me lay
To keep me happy all the day.

And sometimes for an hour or so
I watched my leaden soldiers go,
With different uniforms and drills,
Among the bed-clothes, through the hills;

And sometimes sent my ships in fleets
All up and down among the sheets;
Or brought my trees and houses out,
And planted cities all about.

I was the giant great and still
That sits upon the pillow-hill,
And sees before him, dale and plain,
The pleasant land of counterpane.

counterpane—*a bedspread or quilt*

WINTER-TIME

Late lies the wintry sun a-bed,
A frosty, fiery sleepy-head;
Blinks but an hour or two; and then,
A blood-red orange, sets again.

Before the stars have left the skies,
At morning in the dark I rise;
And shivering in my nakedness,
By the cold candle, bathe and dress.

Close by the jolly fire I sit
To warm my frozen bones a bit;
Or, with a reindeer-sled, explore
The colder countries round the door.

When to go out, my nurse doth wrap
Me in my comforter and cap;
The cold wind burns my face, and blows
Its frosty pepper up my nose.

Black are my steps on silver sod;
Thick blows my frosty breath abroad;
And tree and house, and hill and lake,
Are frosted like a wedding cake.

comforter—*long, knitted scarf*
sod—*turf, grassy ground*

WINDY NIGHTS

Whenever the moon and stars are set,
    Whenever the wind is high,
All night long in the dark and wet,
    A man goes riding by.
Late in the night when the fires are out,
Why does he gallop and gallop about?

Whenever the trees are crying aloud,
    And ships are tossed at sea,
By, on the highway, low and loud,
    By at the gallop goes he.
By at the gallop he goes, and then
By he comes back at the gallop again.

NEST EGGS

Birds all the summer day
    Flutter and quarrel
Here in the arbour-like
    Tent of the laurel.

Here in the fork
    The brown nest is seated;
Four little blue eggs
    The mother keeps heated.

While we stand watching her,
    Staring like gabies,
Safe in each egg are the
    Bird's little babies.

Soon the frail eggs they shall
    Chip, and upspringing
Make all the April woods
    Merry with singing.

Younger than we are,
    O children, and frailer,
Soon in the blue air they'll be,
    Singer and sailor.

We, so much older,
    Taller and stronger,
We shall look down on the
    Birdies no longer.

They shall go flying
    With musical speeches
High overhead in the
    Tops of the beeches.

In spite of our wisdom
    And sensible talking,
We on our feet must go
    Plodding and walking.

arbour—*a shelter of vines,
leaves, or branches*
gabies—*people who are simple
or foolish*
beeches—*trees with smooth
gray bark and small
nuts*

THE WIND

I saw you toss the kites on high
And blow the birds about the sky;
And all around I heard you pass,
Like ladies' skirts across the grass—
 O wind, a-blowing all day long,
 O wind, that sings so loud a song!

I saw the different things you did,
But always you yourself you hid.
I felt you push, I heard you call,
I could not see yourself at all—
 O wind, a-blowing all day long,
 O wind, that sings so loud a song!

O you that are so strong and cold,
O blower, are you young or old?
Are you a beast of field and tree,
Or just a stronger child than me?
 O wind, a-blowing all day long,
 O wind, that sings so loud a song!

FROM A RAILWAY CARRRIAGE

Faster than fairies, faster than witches,
Bridges and houses, hedges and ditches;
And charging along like troops in a battle,
All through the meadows the horses and cattle:
All of the sights of the hill and the plain
Fly as thick as driving rain;
And ever again, in the wink of an eye,
Painted stations whistle by.

Here is a child who clambers and scrambles,
All by himself and gathering brambles;
Here is a tramp who stands and gazes;
And there is the green for stringing the daisies!
Here is a cart runaway in the road
Lumping along with man and load;
And here is a mill and there is a river:
Each a glimpse and gone forever!

A SONG OF THE ROAD

The gauger walked with willing foot,
And aye the gauger played the flute;
And what should Master Gauger play
But Over the hills and far away?

Whene'er I buckle on my pack
And foot it gaily in the track,
O pleasant gauger, long since dead,
I hear you fluting on ahead.

You go with me the self-same way—
The self-same air for me you play;
For I do think and so do you
It is the tune to travel to.

For who would gravely set his face
To go to this or t'other place?
There's nothing under Heav'n so blue
That's fairly worth the travelling to.

On every hand the roads begin,
And people walk with zeal therein;
But wheresoe'er the highways tend,
Be sure there's nothing at the end.

Then follow you, wherever hie
The travelling mountains of the sky.
Or let the streams in civil mode
Direct your choice upon a road;

For one and all, or high or low,
Will lead you where you wish to go;
And one and all go night and day
Over the hills and far away!

gauger—*someone who gauges or measures*
things to make sure they are the
right size
hie—*to go quickly*

45

BLOCK CITY

What are you able to build with your blocks?
Castles and palaces, temples and docks.
Rain may keep raining, and others go roam,
But I can be happy and building at home.

Let the sofa be mountains, the carpet be sea,
There I'll establish a city for me:
A kirk and a mill and a palace beside,
And a harbour as well where my vessels may ride.

Great is the palace with pillar and wall,
A sort of a tower on the top of it all,
And steps coming down in an orderly way
To where my toy vessels lie safe in the bay.

This one is sailing and that one is moored:
Hark to the song of the sailors aboard!
And see, on the steps of my palace, the kings
Coming and going with presents and things!

Now I have done with it, down let it go!
All in a moment the town is laid low.
Block upon block lying scattered and free,
What is there left of my town by the sea?

Yet as I saw it, I see it again,
The kirk and the palace, the ships and the men,
And as long as I live and where'er I may be,
I'll always remember my town by the sea.

kirk—*church*
vessels—*ships and boats*
moor—*to anchor a boat or ship or to make it secure with a line or rope*

REQUIEM

Under the wide and starry sky,
Dig the grave and let me lie.
Glad did I live and gladly die,
   And I laid me down with a will.

This be the verse you grave for me;
Here he lies where he longed to be,
Home is the sailor, home from the sea,
   And the hunter home from the hill.

INDEX